Under My Feet

Snakes

Patricia Whitehouse

Heinemann Library

Chicago, Illinois

© 2004 Heinemann Library
a division of Reed Elsevier Inc.
Chicago, Illinois

Customer Service 888-454-2279
Visit our website at www.heinemannlibrary.com

Designed by Sue Emerson, Heinemann Library; Page layout by Que-Net Media™
Printed and bound in the United States by Lake Book Manufacturing, Inc.
Photo research by Bill Broyles

08 07 06 05 04
10 9 8 7 6 5 4 3 2 1

Library of Congress Cataloging-in-Publication Data
Whitehouse, Patricia, 1958-
  Snakes / Patricia Whitehouse.
     v. cm. – (Under my feet)
Summary: Do snakes live here? – What are snakes? – What do snakes look like? – Where do snakes live? – What do snake homes look like? – How do snakes find their way underground? – How do snakes make their homes? – What is special about snake homes? – When do snakes come out from underground? – Snake home map.
  ISBN 1-4034-4320-3 (HC), 1-4034-4329-7 (Pbk.)
  1. Snakes–Juvenile literature. [1. Snakes.] I. Title.
  QL666.O6W453 2003
  597.96–dc21

                                 2002156757

Acknowledgments
The author and publishers are grateful to the following for permission to reproduce copyright material:
p. 4 Phoebe Dunn/Stock Connection; pp. 5, 12, 13, 16, 17 Jim Merli/Visuals Unlimited; pp. 6, 10, 18, 21 Dwight Kuhn; p. 7 Michael Fogden/Bruce Coleman Inc.; p. 8R Thomas Gula/Visuals Unlimited; p. 8L Gail M. Shumwav/Bruce Coleman Inc.; p. 9 John Sohlden/Visuals Unlimited; p. 11L Corbis; p. 11R C. McIntyre/PhotoLink/Getty Images; p. 14 Littlehales, Bates/Animals Animals/Earth Scenes; p. 15 Stephen J. Krasemann/DRK Photo; p. 18 Ian Beames/Ardea London Ltd.; p. 19 Joe McDonald/Bruce Coleman Inc.; p. 20 John Visser/Bruce Coleman Inc.; p. 23 (row 1, L-R) Jim Merli/Visuals Unlimited, Corbis, Michael Fogden/Bruce Coleman Inc.; (row 2, L-R) Jim Merli/Visuals Unlimited, Michael Fogden/Bruce Coleman Inc.; (row 3) C. McIntyre/PhotoLink/Getty Images; back cover (L-R) Jim Merli/Visuals Unlimited, Michael Fogden/Bruce Coleman Inc.

Illustration on page 22 by Will Hobbs
Cover photograph by William Leonard/DRK Photo

Special thanks to our advisory panel for their help in the preparation of this book:

Alice Bethke, Library Consultant
Palo Alto, CA

Eileen Day, Preschool Teacher
Chicago, IL

Kathleen Gilbert,
Second Grade Teacher
Round Rock, TX

Sandra Gilbert,
Library Media Specialist
Fiest Elementary School
Houston, TX

Jan Gobeille,
Kindergarten Teacher
Garfield Elementary
Oakland, CA

Angela Leeper,
Educational Consultant
Wake Forest, NC

Special thanks to Lee Haines at the Brookfield Zoo for his review of this book.

Some words are shown in bold, **like this.**
You can find them in the picture glossary on page 23.

Contents

Do Snakes Live Here?

When you walk outside, you might not see a snake.

But you might be walking over one.

Some snakes live under your feet.

Their homes are underground.

What Are Snakes?

Snakes are **reptiles**.

Most reptiles come out of eggs.

scale

Reptile bodies are covered with **scales.**

The scales are smooth and dry.

What Do Snakes Look Like?

Snakes have long, thin bodies.

Some snakes have bright colors, and some have dark colors.

Some snakes are as short and thin as a pencil.

This snake is as long as your arms.

Where Do Snakes Live?

Many snakes live underground.

Their homes are called **burrows**.

Some snakes live in **forests**.

Some live in **deserts**.

What Do Snake Homes Look Like?

Snake homes have a **tunnel** and a **den**.

A den is a room at the end of the tunnel.

Some snakes put their eggs in special rooms.

There are two different kinds of snake eggs in this room.

How Do They Find Their Way?

Snakes use their tongues to find their way underground.

Snakes smell with their tongues.

Their tongues can also tell if something is moving nearby.

How Do Snakes Make Their Homes?

Some snakes dig with their heads.

They use their hard heads to push out dirt.

Many snakes dig by wiggling through the dirt.

The dirt gets pushed out with their bodies.

What Is Special About Their Homes?

Sometimes snakes move into empty homes.

These homes were made by other animals, like this rabbit.

Snakes might change these homes.

They might add more **dens** or holes to get out.

When Do Snakes Come Out from Underground?

Some snakes come out to find food.

Many snakes sleep all winter.

They come out of their **burrows** in the spring.

Snake Home Map

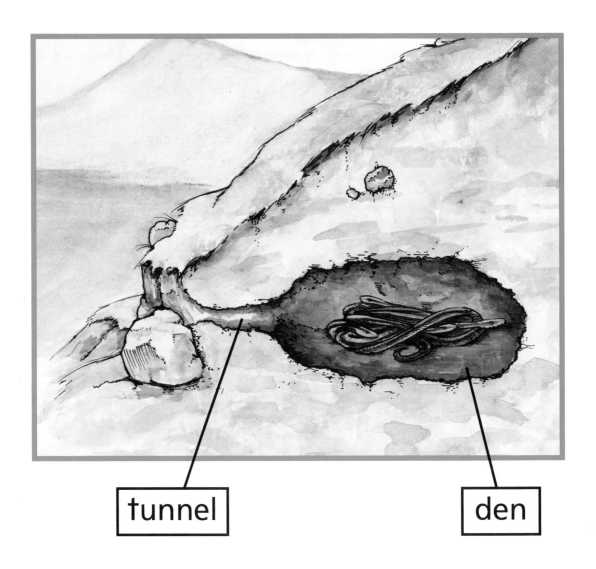

tunnel

den

Picture Glossary

burrow
pages 10, 21

forest
page 11

scales
page 7

den
pages 12, 19,
22

reptile
pages 6, 7

tunnel
pages 12, 22

desert
page 11

Note to Parents and Teachers

Reading for information is an important part of a child's literacy development. Learning begins with a question about something. Help children think of themselves as investigators and researchers by encouraging their questions about the world around them. Each chapter in this book begins with a question. Read the question together. Look at the pictures. Talk about what you think the answer might be. Then read the text to find out if your predictions were correct. Think of other questions you could ask about the topic, and discuss where you might find the answers. Assist children in using the picture glossary and the index to practice new vocabulary and research skills.

! CAUTION: Remind children that it is not a good idea to handle wild animals or insects. Children should wash their hands with soap and water after they touch any animal.

Index